Ten Town Trails
South Devon

Robert Hesketh

Bossiney Books

First published 2014 by
Bossiney Books Ltd, 33 Queens Drive, Ilkley, LS29 9QW
www.bossineybooks.com

ISBN 978-1-906474-44-7

Acknowledgements
The maps are by Graham Hallowell.
All photographs are by the author or from the publishers' own collection.
Printed in Great Britain by R Booth Ltd, Penryn, Cornwall

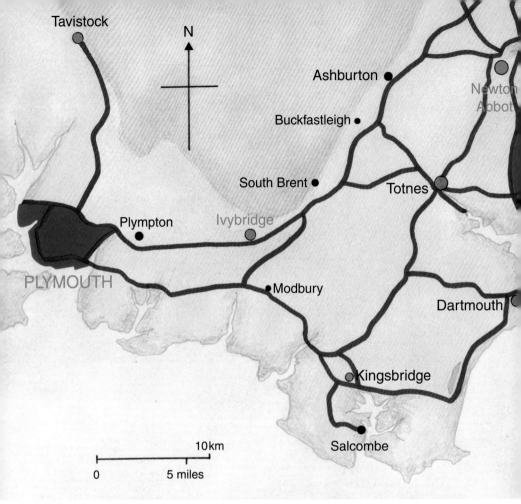

The towns for which trails are provided are labelled in black. Several trails for Plymouth are given in 'Plymouth – a Shortish Guide'

Some other Bossiney books you may find useful

Devon castles
Devon's history
Dartmouth – a shortish guide
Exeter – a shortish guide
Plymouth – a shortish guide
The South Hams – a shortish guide
Really short walks – South Devon
Shortish walks – the south Devon Coast

Tavistock from the railway viaduct

Tavistock

Distance: 3km (2 miles)

Tavistock's character owes much to its previous landowners. It grew around the Benedictine abbey, founded in 974. Under its patronage, Tavistock gained a weekly market. Its prosperity was built on wool and tin and it became a 'stannary town', administering the local tin industry. In 1539 John Russell, ennobled as the first Duke of Bedford, acquired the abbey and its substantial assets when Henry VIII dissolved England's monasteries.

The 19th century Tamar Valley copper boom transformed Tavistock: the population trebled between 1801 and 1861. Using the wealth from their mines, the Dukes of Bedford redeveloped the town centre and the south-western approaches to the town. On the outskirts, the Bedfords built model houses such as Fitzford Cottages for their workers.

Start from Plymouth Road car park. Facing the river, turn left and follow the path past the Abbey Still House, where the monks distilled herbs to make medicines. Continue to Abbey Bridge, a 1763 replacement for the medieval bridge: it was widened in 1860 when the railway, then new, brought increased traffic. Cross the bridge, turn right and follow the path along the other bank to an iron bridge.

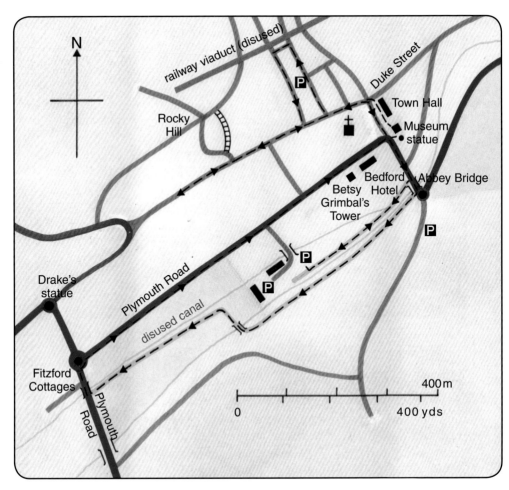

Cross over, then cross the park to the Tavistock Canal, built in 1817 to carry mineral ore from Tavistock Wharf to Morwellham Quay, 7 km distant on the Tamar. Turn left and follow the canal to Plymouth Road. On the far side of the road are Fitzford Cottages. Turn right to the Drake Memorial (1883). Sir Francis Drake, born at Crowndale near Tavistock, was one of Elizabethan England's most forceful characters, winning fame for his circumnavigation of the globe 1577-80 and as second in command against the Spanish Armada of 1588.

Turn right up Plymouth Road. Nearly opposite the church is the 19th century vicarage with 'Betsy Grimbal's Tower' in its front garden. Next is the Bedford Hotel, which began as a merchant's house on the site of the Abbey's refectory in 1725 and was converted into a hotel in the mid 19th century.

'Betsy Grimbal's Tower' (probably a corruption of Blessed Grimbald, a 9th century saint) – all that remains of the 15th century Abbot's Lodging and the Abbey's western gatehouse

From the genuine medieval to the Victorian version – Tavistock Town Hall, in castellated gothic style, with a passage leading through to a market area

Cross Plymouth Road to St Eustachius's. In the churchyard is the one remaining arch of the Abbey's cloisters. These adjoined the once magnificent Abbey church of 1318. St Eustachius's is mainly 16th century and built of the local grey-green Hurdwick stone which is such a feature of Tavistock.

Cross to Bedford Square, where Francis, 7th Duke of Bedford, surveys his work from a statue (1864) cast in bronze with ores from the fantastically productive Tamar Valley mines. Bedford Square is mainly castellated Victorian Gothic. Again in Hurdwick stone, it incorporates medieval elements in the court and police station and, most notably, the medieval gatehouse with its fine 12th century arches, which was remodelled by John Foulston in the 1820s.

Tavistock's Pannier Market which has a range of stalls from food to crafts, clothes, antiques, second-hand books and bric-a-brac

At the statue, turn left and go through the archway. On the left is the Tourist Information Centre. Opposite is the Museum, with exhibits on mining, agriculture and the railway. It also has a video about Tavistock Abbey, architectural drawings showing the 19th century rebuilding of Tavistock and a huge collection of local photographs.

Divert right to visit the Pannier Market, purpose built in the 1860s with gabled roof and broad arches. Return to Bedford Square. Turn right then left into West Street.

Take the second right into Market Street. Continue to the Union Inn, from where you will have a view of the 1889 railway viaduct. Just beyond the Inn, you might divert left to join the signed Viaduct Walk up a steep stepped path – note the plaque explaining Tavistock's railway history on the wall to the left of the sign. Turn right at the top of the path and then right onto the viaduct as signed to gain an aerial view of the town.

Retrace your steps to the Union Inn. Continue ahead down King Street. At the junction of West Street and King Street is the 1835 Corn Exchange with its Doric columns. Continue up West Street, which has a fine medley of 18th and 19th century frontages. On the right as you ascend the slope is Rocky Hill – the main road to Launceston in the days before wheeled transport, and only bypassed around 1822.

When you reach the top of the slope, retrace your steps down West Street. Turn right across Bedford Square. Opposite the Bedford statue is the Abbey Chapel, once the site of the Abbot's Hall. Turn right by Abbey Bridge; retrace your steps by the bankside path to the car park.

Plympton's Butterwalk

Plympton

Distance: 2km (1¹/₄ miles)

Plympton predates Plymouth and was once a more significant port, but it has been part of the city since 1967 and has expanded greatly.

Happily, Plympton retains an ancient core of great character with many listed buildings. After the Conquest, Richard de Redvers established Plympton Castle and Bishop Warlewast the Augustinian Priory (1121). Medieval Plympton prospered and gained its charter in 1242, becoming in 1328 a stannary town, where tin was weighed and assayed. In the 19th century Plympton's industries declined and it lost its two MPs in the Great Reform of 1832.

Start from Mudge Way car park. Walk downhill to Living Well Church. Turn right and immediately left into Dark Street Lane and follow it to its end. Turn left into Underwood Road and follow it round into Fore Street, a delightful mix of irregular facades, many of them Georgian, with medieval burgage plots behind. Number 9, the Rectory, is early 18th century and The Foresters Arms 17th/18th century, but remodelled in the late 19th.

Centre stage is the 17th century Guildhall. Its upper floor rests on granite columns. The Treby name and arms and the 1688 and 1696 datestones are quite distinct. To the right, the arcaded buildings are a

7

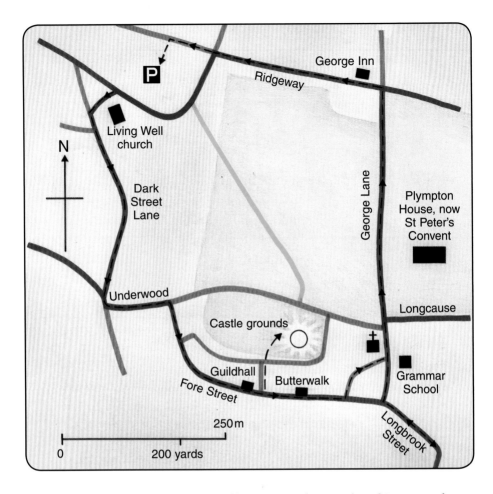

modest version of the butterwalks at Totnes (page 20) and Dartmouth (page 28), and are thought to be late 16th/early 17th century.

Turn left up Castle Lane beside the Guildhall to visit Plympton Castle. Climb to the top of the motte for a splendid view over the town. Plympton House is certainly best seen from the motte. Sir Christopher Wren, who was MP for Plympton as well as an outstanding architect, is said to have designed it. Lord Chief Justice Treby began it and it was completed by his son in 1720.

Return to Fore Street and turn left past the Butterwalk. Turn left into Church road. The London Inn is an 18th century coaching inn with a remarkable collection of military (mainly naval) insignia. Continue past St Maurice's. The church, noted for its tall tower, has a memorial to Plympton's most famous son, Sir Joshua Reynolds. The

Top: Plympton Castle was first raised around 1100 as a castle mound (motte) and large outer courtyard (bailey). It was besieged and razed by King Stephen in 1136. What remains today may be from the rebuilding of the 1140s, when Baldwin de Redvers recovered his estates and was made Earl of Devon by Stephen's arch enemy, Empress Matilda.

Below: Plympton House, seen from the motte

great portrait painter was born in Plympton in 1723 and educated at the Grammar School, where his father was Master. Continue along Church Street to the former Grammar School (not open to the public). Built in 1664, its first floor rests on Tuscan columns.

Divert right then left into Longbrook Street, which has a pleasing range of mainly 18th/19th century buildings. Retrace your steps and head past the Grammar School up equally pleasing George Lane.

At its end, turn left onto Ridgeway by the George Hotel, a slate-hung 18th century coaching inn. At a mini-roundabout, continue ahead, and follow Ridgeway past shops to St Stephen's Place. Turn left here past the Augustinian Priory arch, back to the car park.

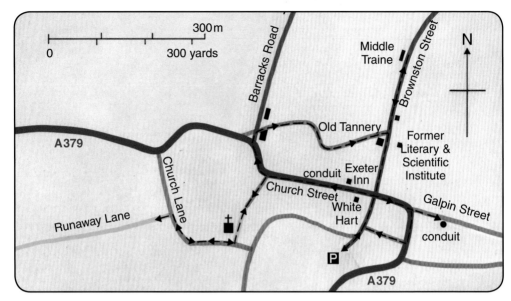

Modbury

Distance: 2km (1 1/4 miles)

Modbury's Old English name signifies a meeting place at a defensible position. In 1155 Modbury gained a charter for regular markets and fairs. Prosperity has left Modbury a fine architectural heritage.

Start from Poundwell Street car park. Head up Poundwell Street to the main road. The market cross and shambles (meat market) were sited here where four streets meet. Turn left by the White Hart, built in 1827. Cross over to the Exeter Inn. Modbury's oldest inn, it dates from the 16th/early 17th century, but with considerable later alterations. The facade is pseudo-timber-frame, whilst the interior has very low ceilings and a 16th century type stone fire hood. Head up the hill (Church Street), where many houses have attractive 18th and 19th century facades and dignified and handsome doorways. Notice the conduit given by Nicholas Trist in 1708.

Turn left at the War Memorial towards St George's. Although the church is mainly 14th century, its broach spire was rebuilt after a lightning strike in 1621. Leave the churchyard by the West Gate. Follow the cobbled path beside the lane around the bend. Runaway Lane is on the left – a plaque explains the origin of the name. Retrace your steps through the churchyard to the War Memorial.

Turn left up Church Street, then first right. On your right is Manor

House. Possibly 16th/17th century, it was modified later. The characteristically Victorian school dates from 1881. You could make a 350 m each way diversion from here down Barracks Road to see the austere remains of the 1794 barracks.

Otherwise turn right and follow Back Street to its junction with Brownston Street. The Old Tannery, on your right as you enter Brownston Street, was once a warehouse. Opposite is the former Modbury Literary and Scientific Institute, where subjects 'likely to excite anger, passion or a factious party spirit' were banned.

Turn left up Brownston Street past the 18th century Modbury Inn with its mounting block. On the right is a water conduit of 1708. Continue uphill. Traine has a long and imposing early Victorian colonnade, fronting an earlier house of 1780.

Retrace your steps down Brownston Street. Turn left at the main road into Broad Street. On your left the old market bell hangs from the wall of the former Bell Inn. At the start of Modbury's May Fair a glove filled with flowers is placed above the bell.

When the main road heads right, continue up Galpin Street to another conduit. Retrace your steps down Galpin Street. Turn left on the main road. Walk past Red Devon Court and turn right down steps past 17th century Poundwell House to the start.

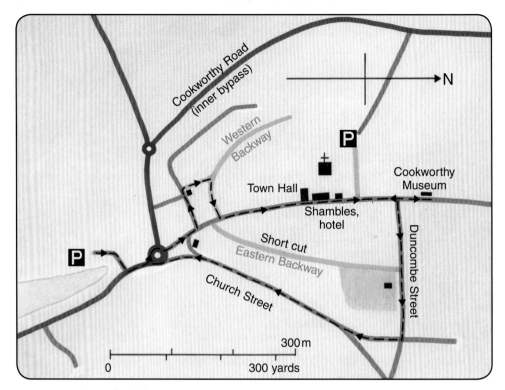

Kingsbridge

Distance: 1.6 km (1 mile)

Kingsbridge enjoys a favoured position at the head of its estuary. Like Salcombe (page 15) it owed much of its prosperity to maritime trade and shipbuilding. Its name derives from the bridge connecting the royal estates of West Alvington and Chillington, as recorded in AD 962. Kingsbridge gained its market in 1219 and remains the market town for a wide area of the South Hams.

Start at the Quay Car Park, built on reclaimed land. The Quay is home to a variety of pleasure boats and yachts, but the cargo ships that exported cider, corn, carriages and stone are gone.

Date's Shipyard built elegant schooners for the Azores fruit run and large paddle steamers, including the *Express*. From 1885 until 1893, this took passengers from Kingsbridge and Salcombe to Plymouth.

Down the estuary, 22 lime kilns survive. They were fed with limestone brought by barge from Plymouth. The Quay's commercial decline began with the arrival of the railway from South Brent in 1893. The railway's last whistle was blown in 1963.

Cut across the Town Square and head up Fore Street by the 19th century Quay Inn. Turn left into Mill Street and right by the Hermitage Inn up Squeezebelly Lane – its narrowness justifies its name! Turn right into Western Backway, where the leat powered the mills in Mill Street. Along with the leat in Eastern Backway, it bounded old Kingsbridge like a town wall.

Turn left up Fore Street. Most of the handsome slate-hung houses have 18th or early 19th century facades, but their narrow frontages betray their origins as medieval burgage plots. A 15th century cruck roof was discovered in one, and there are several medieval courtyards, some accessed by narrow alleys.

Continue to the Town Hall (1850) with its fine clock (1875). Next is the Shambles. The present building dates from 1796 but stands on granite piers dating from 1586, which form a loggia similar to those at Dartmouth, Totnes and Plympton. They were remodelled in 1796, when the market in the middle of the street and the 18th century water conduits were removed.

St Edmund's church is distinguished by its 13th century crossing tower and spire. On the exterior wall is a piece of local doggerel composed for his demise by 'Bone' Phillips (1793):

Here I lie at the chancel door
Here I lie because I'm poor
The further in the more you'll pay
Here I lie as warm as they.

Continue along Fore Street to the King's Arms Hotel. Built as a coaching inn in 1775, it has a high entrance arch leading to former stables.

Higher up Fore Street is the Cookworthy Museum, a distinguished 17th century stone building with mullioned windows. It commemorates two Kingsbridgians. Thomas Crispin, fuller, founded the Grammar School here in 1670, whilst William Cookworthy discovered china clay in Cornwall and took out patents for its use in hard paste porcelain. Museum exhibits include archive photographs, grammar school graffiti dating to 1735, shipwrights' and foundry tools, period costumes and a very large collection of agricultural machinery.

Now retrace your steps and turn left into Duncombe Street. Either take the short cut, turning right along an alleyway (Eastern Backway) to the Quay, or take the first road turning right (Belle Vue Road) then follow Church Street down to the Quay.

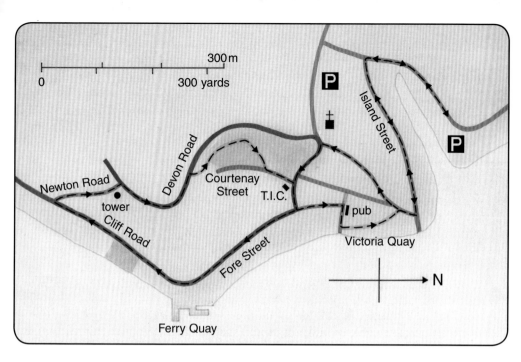

Salcombe

Distance: 2.5km (1¹/2 miles)

Salcombe first developed as a port and shipbuilding centre. The 19th century, when Salcombe shipyards built everything from small coastal craft to 500 ton barquentines, was a boom period. Local fast schooners called 'Salcombe Fruiters' traded to Portugal, Spain and the Azores; larger Salcombe ships plied the oceans to the West Indies for sugar and fruit, to Newfoundland for fish and China for tea.

Meanwhile, Salcombe's superb scenery and mild climate increasingly drew visitors and settlers, especially after the railway reached Kingsbridge in 1893. Cargo ships gave way to pleasure craft and yachts. Salcombe's shipwrights adapted their skills to the new trade.

Start from Creek car park – or from the TIC (see * on next page) if using the park and ride service. Turn left out of Creek car park and left again into Island Street, where boatyards have been built on reclaimed land. On the left, the mainly 19th century stone and clapboard buildings in Thorning Street were once stables and a slaughterhouse.

Near the end of Island Street, turn right into Church Street. The houses on the right were built for coastguards. The larger houses for the senior coastguards are near the foot of the hill. Holy Trinity church was built in 1843 to replace the medieval chapel of ease.

Turn left downhill to the Tourist Information Centre*. This building was originally a semi-religious teetotal establishment to guard sailors from the dreaded drink, and the upper half displays stained glass windows. The lower half is the Maritime Museum.

Continue down Market Street and turn right into Fore Street. Despite modern shop fronts and some Second World War bomb damage, this is the heart of old Salcombe and was once crowded with shipyards and even more houses than today.

Opposite the 18th century Kings Arms is an ornate iron tap topped by a notice prohibiting fish cleaning – one of three public taps which served the town between 1835 and 1895, when mains water arrived.

Next is the 18th century Victoria Inn and opposite it Normandy Way, with a plaque commemorating the American servicemen who embarked from here with 66 US Navy ships and many auxiliaries to play their part in D Day, June 1944.

Ferry to South Sands and excursion to Overbecks

At this point, you may board the South Sands ferry (seasonal). The 2km journey to this most attractive beach includes excellent views of Salcombe and Salcombe Castle. A fifteen minute uphill walk from South Sands leads to Overbecks (National Trust, 01548 842893) with its sub-tropical gardens and superb views: with your back to the estuary, follow the lane left and seaward.

Continue along Fore Street past the former Shipwright's Arms where shipyard workers could buy drink directly from their wages with tokens. Divert left down steps to visit the 18th century Ferry Inn, named from the East Portlemouth ferry, which has plied from the pier for centuries past.

Return to Fore Street, which becomes Cliff Road. Pass Cliff House gardens and turn sharp right up Newton Road. At the top of Newton Road is a small castellated tower (c.1795), belonging to the Old Watch House. Turn right down Devon Road, from where there are attractive views over the rooftops of Salcombe.

Turn right down a flight of steps and slightly left into Courtenay Park. Follow the path through the park, down to Courtenay Street

Above: The view across the estuary from Newton Road

Below: The Fortescue Inn is named from an old Devon family. Col. Sir Edmond Fortescue and Col. Henry Champernowne recruited two regiments from the South Hams to fight for Charles I. Sir Edmond commanded Salcombe Castle near North Sands. He and his 63 men resisted attack for several weeks, but were obliged to surrender in May 1646, thus ending the Civil War in mainland Devon

and the TIC. Follow Market Street down to Fore Street again, but this time turn left. At the Fortescue Inn, turn right down Union Street. The Lifeboat Shop has wonderful scale models of lifeboats and photographs to tell the proud history of Salcombe's lifeboats. The Custom House opposite has a crest over the door. Retrace your steps and turn right under the arch before you reach the Fortescue. Above is a former sail loft, now an artist's studio.

Follow the path by Victoria Quay, with its attractive terrace. Ships were careened here to remove weed below the waterline and copper-bottomed to protect them from Teredo worms. Opposite is the site of Wrecker Distin's yard, where ships were broken for scrap.

Turn left into Island Street and retrace your steps to the car park.

Dartmouth

Distance: 2.4km (1¹/₂ miles) excluding diversions to Kingswear and Dartmouth castle. Within the town there are some short but steep slopes and steps

Recognising a superb natural haven when they saw one, the Normans first developed port facilities on the higher ground north and south of Dartmouth's present harbour area. Medieval Dartmouth built its wealth on exporting wool, wheat and fish and importing Bordeaux wine. Trade and war often overlapped and Dartmouth's merchants turned readily to privateering in their armed ships. Dartmouth was crucial to national defence and its first castle was built in 1388. This was later modernised and strengthened, then augmented by Kingswear and Bearscove castles. All three survive.

Meanwhile, the Dartmouth merchants reclaimed land from the estuary mudflats and built some of the best timber-framed 16th and 17th century houses in Devon. Many fine buildings were added in the 18th and 19th centuries, making it a very rewarding town to explore.

A much fuller account can be found in another Bossiney book, *Dartmouth: a Shortish Guide*, available in the town.

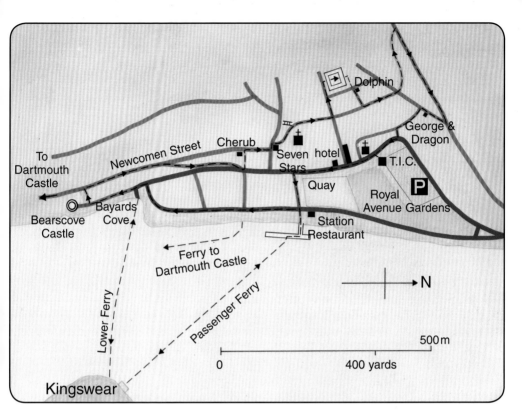

Start from the Tourist Information Centre, where the Memorial Engine honours Dartmouth's pioneering mechanical engineer, Thomas Newcomen. Cross the road to the church, built in 1895 to celebrate non-conformist preacher John Flavel (1630-1691), Vicar of Townstal until his ejection under Charles II's intolerant regime in 1662.

Opposite the church are the Royal Avenue Gardens, laid out as a formal garden in Victoria's reign. The site had been reclaimed from mudflats in the 1670s to provide additional moorings for ships. For 200 years it remained an island, linked to the Quay by a bridge.

Duke Street contains the grandest Butterwalk in Devon, if not in England. A series of granite piers support the upper floors, providing a covered market. Four splendid timber-framed houses built between 1628 and 1640 (and well restored after wartime bomb damage) form the Butterwalk, which reflects the prosperity which the maritime trade, especially in Newfoundland cod and Devon cloth, brought to Dartmouth. When the Butterwalk was built, ships moored at the rear and discharged their cargoes directly.

The Butterwalk's upper floors are profusely carved, whilst the interiors have wonderful plasterwork, best seen in the Sloping Deck Restaurant. Dartmouth Museum at the near end of the Butterwalk also has excellent plasterwork ceilings and linenfold panelling. Its pole staircase uses a recycled ship's mast.

Head back to the Quay and turn right along it. Built between 1584 and 1640 over former mudflats, the Quay and its neighbouring streets retain Devon's best collection of 17th century merchants' houses – and some flamboyant Victorian imitations, with pargeting, slate-hanging and iron cresting, far outdoing the originals.

The Royal Castle Hotel began in 1639 as two merchants' houses, though some of the roof beams may be older. By 1777 the two houses had been combined, with a brewhouse and stables at the rear. The remarkable top-lit staircase hall with its magnificent bell board was built in the old courtyard in 1835, when a third floor and the present facade were all added. When a new turnpike road was built, the Castle prospered as a coaching inn and later restyled itself as a hotel.

Top: The Royal Dart Hotel, Kingswear, which began as the Plume of Feathers, then became the Station Hotel in 1864. As the Dart Yacht Club met here, it was renamed the Yacht Hotel and added 'Royal' to its name after Queen Victoria patronised the Dartmouth Regatta – still the town's major annual event.

Below: Dartmouth's Custom House Quay, with the Lower (vehicle) Ferry

Continue along the Quay. The premises at the junction with Fairfax Place are 17th century, whilst York House at the junction with South Embankment was built in 1893. Opposite is the Station Restaurant. When the Paignton to Kingswear railway opened in 1864, passengers completed the journey to Dartmouth by ferry – thus the station never saw a train, though it did sell railway tickets.

To enjoy unparalleled views of the river, take the Kingswear ferry from here and visit the station, preserved by the Dart Valley Railway Company, which has also preserved the stations through to Paignton. It operates a regular steam hauled service there through the season on this outstandingly beautiful route.

Return to Dartmouth by the passenger ferry. Walk seaward along South Embankment. From here, you may take a short and very scenic boat trip to Dartmouth Castle. Alternatively, walk to the castle, a pleasant near level route of 2.2km (1 1/3 miles). See instructions below (*).

At the far end of the Embankment is a Russian cannon, captured in the Crimean War. Bear right, then left to Bayard's Cove Inn, medieval in origin though altered in later centuries. Walk past the Devon Arms onto cobbled Bayard's Cove, lined with attractive 17th to early 19th century houses. The grandest is the Old Customs House of 1739. Gull Cottage bears an 18th century fire insurance mark.

At the far end of Bayard's Cove is Bearscove Castle, a small artillery fort with eleven gunports built in 1510 to protect the quays. On returning from the castle turn left almost immediately up Castle Steps to Newcomen Road. To visit Dartmouth Castle (*), turn left and follow the riverside streets.

Otherwise, turn right. Newcomen Road is lined with attractive Georgian houses which have fine views of the harbour and river mouth. Keep right into Lower Street when the road forks. At the bottom is the former Harbour Bookshop. Another plaque recalls its founder, Christopher Robin Milne, son of AA Milne and hero of the *Christopher Robin* stories – which he refused to stock.

Walk ahead towards Fairfax Place and more exuberant Victorian half-timbering. Turn left up Horn Hill Steps to the Cherub. Built *c.*1380, it is the oldest secular building in Dartmouth and its only complete medieval house. There is a single room on each jettied floor and the pole staircase (like the museum's) is made from a ship's mast.

Turn right along Higher Street to see more medieval houses on the right (undergoing restoration after fire damage at the time of writing). These were originally the shambles (butchers' shops) at the medieval heart of Dartmouth. The stocks and pillory provided further amusement.

Turn left and immediately right past the Seven Stars to St Saviour's. Built in 1372, the church has a beautifully carved and painted rood screen (1496). John Hawley's 1408 memorial brass is preserved under the chancel carpet. Turn right out of the church into St Saviour's Square and left up Collaford Steps. At the top is a notice banning wheelbarrows and hand carts.

Walk back down the steps and follow Anzac Street to Duke Street. Turn left into Victoria Road and first right to enter the Old Market (1828). On the far side of the Old Market is Market Square. Head

Left: The opulently ornamented pulpit of St Saviour's church
Right: The Cherub Inn, built c.1380

across the Square and into Union Street to the right of the Dolphin Inn. Turn left into Foss Street, with its 17th and 18th century buildings. Continue to the far end of the street. Cross opposite 18th century Broadstone House and follow the steps up Brown's Hill.

This was the packhorse route to Townstal – before Victoria Road was built in 1823, there was no route for wheeled traffic into Dartmouth. Continue to the end. Bear right up steps. Turn right onto Clarence Hill, a medieval street, and enjoy the views.

At the bottom of Clarence Hill, turn right into Broadstone to the George and Dragon. On the left is Undercliff, the original shoreline. Continue along Broadstone and turn first left at Zion Place into Mayor's Avenue. The Tourist Information Centre is straight ahead.

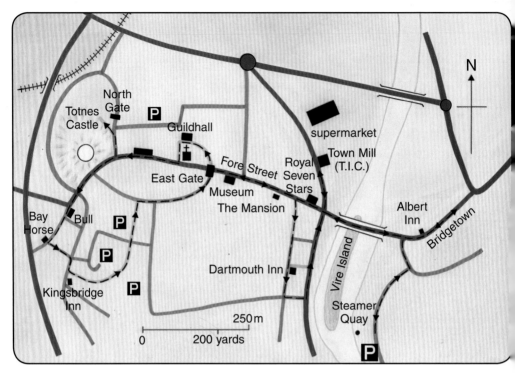

Totnes

Distance: 3 km (2 miles)

Totnes enjoyed a good defensive position, strategically placed on a ridge overlooking the lowest bridging point on the Dart, with direct access to the sea and maritime trade. The Anglo-Saxons established a mint and a fortified settlement here, elements of which can be traced in the town's ramparts.

Shortly after the Conquest, the Normans built the first Totnes Castle. Using a natural rocky knoll, they raised it even higher with earth and stones and erected a 3.4 m high timber tower to overawe the defeated English. This was replaced in 1336 by the stone castle we see today which still dominates Totnes.

By Domesday (1086), Totnes was a port with 110 burgesses and a total population of about 500, making it a place of importance by medieval standards. Its status was further raised in 1206 when King John granted it a charter, making it a free town. A stone bridge soon followed, encouraging the wool trade upon which much of Totnes's fortune was built.

Cloth exports went via Dartmouth and were mainly despatched to French ports from Rouen to La Rochelle and to the Iberian Peninsula. Tudor Totnes became Devon's second wealthiest town, after Exeter.

Rich Totnes cloth merchants have left a remarkable heritage of Elizabethan buildings in Fore and High Streets. Several retain their steep gabled roofs and overhanging jetties, though others are partly disguised by Georgian facades. In High Street, the Butterwalk (first recorded in 1532) is an arcaded walkway presenting a medley of 16th and 17th century houses.

Start from Steamer Quay car park – where you will disembark if you arrive from Dartmouth by boat. Retrace your route up Steamer Quay Road to a junction. Turn left and divert right opposite Seymour Terrace for 100 m to see the Albert Inn and other old Bridgetown houses.

Retrace your steps past Seymour Terrace and continue over Totnes Bridge, built by Charles Fowler in 1828. Divert left to explore Vire Island, a small riverside park with good views of former warehouses now converted to apartments. Baltic Wharf, where timber imports were offloaded until the early 1990s, is now occupied by boatyards and riverside apartments.

Return to the bridge. Turn left and then right at the Royal Seven Stars to visit the Town Mill, which houses both the Tourist Information Centre and the Totnes Image Bank – a fascinating archive of over 40,000 local period photographs. Although much altered, the mill building dates to 1588 and its machinery, restored in the 1990s, still turns.

Retrace your steps to the Royal Seven Stars, a splendid late 17th century inn. Its courtyard was later roofed over and the present porch was added around 1825 when the front was rebuilt. Opposite the Royal Seven Stars is the memorial to William Wills, Totnesian explorer of the Australian outback.

Head up Fore Street. Number 36, 'the Mansion', a large Georgian brick building, was formerly King Edward VI Grammar School. Opposite and a little higher up the street is the Brutus Stone. Part of local legend, it has been the gathering place for civic meetings possibly since the Saxon Witan (council).

Fore Street has several 16/17th century merchants' houses, including numbers 50, 52 and 54. Totnes Museum (number 70) is a particularly good example of a tall, gabled Elizabethan timber framed building, with its characteristic courtyard construction and carved,

The Totnes Guildhall, which is open to the public and includes a courtroom, a jail and many historic artefacts

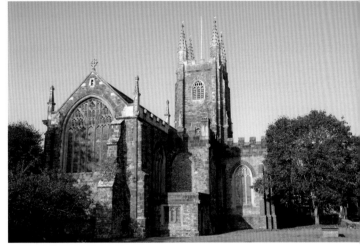

St Mary's Church, formerly the Benedictine priory church

overhanging jetties. The rooms have a variety of local history exhibits and are furnished in Elizabethan style, the forehall and kitchen being particularly interesting. Outside is the Elizabethan herb garden.

Continue up Fore Street to the arch of East Gate. Medieval Totnes was a walled town with three gates. North Gate by the Castle and East Gate, enlarged in 1837 and reconstructed after a fire in 1992, survive.

Beyond East Gate, Fore Street becomes High Street. Numbers 1 and 10 are Elizabethan with later additions. Number 14 (Barclay's Bank at the time of writing) dates from 1585 and bears a plaque recalling that Ann Ball lived here and was married in 1586 to Sir Thomas Bodley, founder of Oxford's Bodleian Library.

Return to East Gate and take the path on the north side. The steps lead up to the Ramparts Walk. Follow it around to the Guildhall, which stands on the site of the Benedictine Priory of St Mary. It dates from 1553, was reconstructed in 1624 and much altered in 1829.

St Mary's was formerly the Benedictine Priory Church. Rebuilt in local red sandstone in the 15th century, its Beer stone rood screen was added in 1460 by Totnes Corporation.

Opposite St Mary's, 28 High Street was formerly the Totnes Theatre. Early 18th century, it is distinguished by grotesque masks on its facade. Turn right up High Street. Beyond the 1960s Civic Hall and market place, and in strong contrast, are the 16/17th century arcaded buildings known as the Poultry Walk. The arcaded walkway opposite is the Butterwalk, a name shared with the Butterwalks in Dartmouth (page 20) and Plympton (page 7). Number 33 is 16th century, but number 43 is 14th/early 15th century, with 16th century remodelling.

Turn right down Castle Street to visit Totnes Castle and see North Gate. Retrace your steps to High Street and turn right into the Narrows, where West Gate once stood. Follow the Narrows past the 19th century Bull Inn, which derives its name from the small square opposite called the Rotherfold, where livestock was sold.

Reaching the early 19th century Bay Horse Inn, turn left into a small street, The Lamb. Turn first right. Just before the Kingsbridge Inn (c.1684 and reputedly the oldest inn in Totnes), turn left into a narrow lane signed HISTORIC LEECHWELLS. The well has three granite troughs and gained its name from the water's supposed medicinal qualities – 'leech' was a medieval term for a physician. It was cared for by wardens, two burgesses being appointed for this purpose in 1444.

Turn left and follow the path downhill and then left towards the car park. Cross a minor road and continue on the path. Reaching South Street, turn right and follow it (with the medieval town wall on its north side) back to East Gate. Turn right and retrace your steps down Fore Street, past the Mansion.

Just before reaching the Seven Stars, turn right into an alley leading into Ticklemore Street. Walk past the early 19th century Dartmouth Inn. Turn left at the junction and left again into The Plains, which has a pleasing mix of buildings mainly from the 18th and 19th centuries. Those on the right are the frontages of the buildings (several former warehouses) viewed earlier on this tour from Vire Island. Reaching the Wills Monument, turn right over the bridge and retrace your steps to Steamer Quay

Top: Totnes Castle (English Heritage, admission charge, 01803 864406) is a textbook motte and bailey fortification. The keep, with its crenellated battlements pierced by arrowslits, still dominates the skyline, and is the highest point in Totnes. From here there is a fine view of the town's ramparts and medieval street pattern.

Middle: Totnes market, with the Butterwalk beyond

The Royal Seven Stars Hotel, a splendid late 17th century inn. Its courtyard was later roofed over and the present porch was added around 1825 when the front was rebuilt.

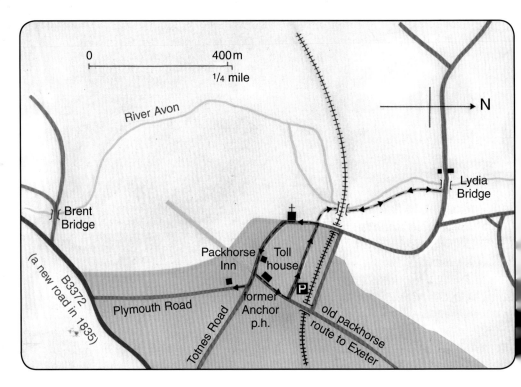

South Brent

Distance: 1.6km (1 mile)

Sheltering beneath Brent Hill, South Brent's narrow streets were once busy with packhorse traffic, and with coaches after 1820, when the Exeter-Plymouth turnpikes were improved. The mainline railway arrived in 1848. It remains, but Brent station is no more. By-passed since 1835, the village has a pleasingly tranquil air today.

Start from the signed car park beside the former railway station in Station Yard. Turn right. Walk to a junction. Turn left and almost immediately right onto PUBLIC FOOTPATH. Follow this under the railway bridge and beside the boulder-strewn river Avon to Lydia Bridge (photograph opposite) with its attractive waterfall.

Like Brent Bridge south of the village, Lydia Bridge probably dates from the late 17th century in its present form. Both bridges bore strings of packhorses, the HGVs of their time, each loaded with panniers mounted on wooden frames. Packhorses travelled in teams of up to forty and continued to carry most of Devon's goods traffic until superseded by wheeled transport in the early 19th century. Note the sign

on the upstream parapet, with its warning to drivers of 'locomotives'.

Retrace your steps downstream to the road. Turn right to visit St Petroc's. The tower and carved sandstone font are both Norman, the rest of the church is mainly 14th and 15th century. Points of interest include the ancient south door with its sanctuary ring; the village stocks; medieval and Tudor chests and a Victorian funeral bier.

Turn right out of the churchyard. Opposite is Wellington Square with its Jubilee Memorial. Follow Church Street as it curves left.

Walk past the Methodist Church (1812) to the Toll House, with its 1889 toll board for markets and fairs. The late 18th/early 19th century Toll House is open to the public and has plaques describing South Brent's history.

Continue ahead past the crossroads and fork right into Plymouth Road. The Packhorse Inn had stables and a forge at the rear. It retains a huge stone fireplace and an interesting collection of local period photographs.

Retrace your steps and turn right into Station Road by the former Anchor Hotel, now a shop. This solid, attractive 19th century building has an impressive roof porch standing on granite piers. Continue past the Oak and turn left into the car park.

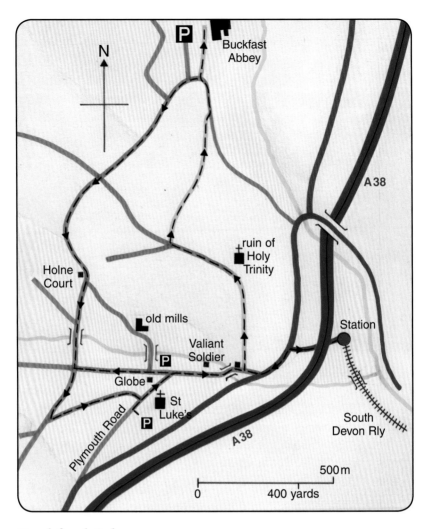

Buckfastleigh

Distance: 1.5 km (1 mile) to explore the town centre. You may then choose to walk to the other points of interest by way of pavements, footpaths and lanes, but this adds 3.5 km (2¼ miles) to the route. Alternatively, use the driving directions (page 35).

The town's centre, sensitively restored and enhanced in the 1990s, retains much of the medieval street layout and a pleasing medley of buildings, mainly from the 17th to the 19th centuries. It grew because of the wool trade, originally fostered by Buckfast Abbey.

The Abbey was established in 1018 and became a Cistercian House

around 1148. The Cistercians' large flocks provided wool for the spinners and weavers of the town, which gained a weekly market in 1353 and prospered through a variety of local industries, notably woollens, quarrying, mining and tanning. There were 700 looms here in 1838, more than in any other Devon town.

Buckfastleigh's Lower Town and Higher Town were linked via the development of Chapel Street in the 19th century. The Hamlyn family, philanthropic mill owners, fostered the industrial, social and religious life of the community. In the 1920s the Co-operative Wholesale Society bought the Hamlyn Mills. These massive buildings still dominate the eastern side of town and are used by several businesses.

Start from the Victoria Woodholme car park on Plymouth Road. Turn right past St Luke's. This starkly modern church was opened in 2002, a replacement for Holy Trinity, severely damaged by arsonists in 1992.

Continue past the White Hart to the Globe Inn. Turn left into Chapel Street. Beyond the car park on the right are the old mill buildings, originally powered by water from the river Mardle. Divert right for a closer view. Return to Chapel Street. Numbers 26-29 are late 17th/early 18th century weavers' cottages. Their tentering lofts are similar to those in Ashburton. Wet cloth was stretched on tenterhooks. The wooden slats allowed currents of air to pass and dry the material.

Hamlyn House, the most impressive of Buckfastleigh's mills

The Valiant Soldier

The Valiant Soldier dates from at least 1747 and probably adopted its present name during the Napoleonic Wars. When it closed in 1965 its owners left it completely unchanged, hoarding the everyday objects of their lives. It has been meticulously restored and offers a wonderful and rare insight into recent social history.

Continue to the junction with Market Street, the start of Higher Town and the site of Buckfastleigh's former markets. Divert right down Market Street past a mix of houses from the 17th to the 19th centuries. Beside the river Mardle are the remains of a launder, carrying water to power the waterwheels. Retrace your steps up Market Street. Continue up narrow Crest Hill and left down Bossell Road past the school and the Town Hall, built in 1887 and enlarged in 1924.

Turn left opposite St Luke's. Turn right by the Globe Inn into Fore Street. Like Market and Chapel Streets, this has a pleasing medley of buildings. Some are slate-hung in characteristically West Country style, some have exposed masonry. Particularly pleasing is the Kings Arms (c.1820) and opposite it the Valiant Soldier, sharing premises with Buckfastleigh Museum and TIC.

After visiting the Valiant Soldier, bear left (signed STEAM RAILWAY) into Station Road. Continue past attractive early 19th century houses. Cross the river bridge and continue to a long flight of stone steps on the left, leading up to Holy Trinity Church.

From the foot of the steps, follow either the driving or the walking directions below.

Driving directions

Retrace your route along Station Road, Fore Street and Plymouth Road. Drive down Plymouth Road. Turn left onto the B3380 for 1 km (2/3 mile). Turn right, SOUTH DEVON RAILWAY BUTTERFLY AND OTTER SANCTUARY. After visiting these attractions, return to the B3380. Turn right to a mini roundabout. Take the first left for BUCKFAST ABBEY. Leaving the abbey's car park, turn right and uphill, BUCKFASTLEIGH. At the crest of the hill, turn left at the crossroads and follow the lane to Holy Trinity. Drive back to the crossroads and retrace your route.

Walking directions

Follow Station Road to the B3380 (Dartbridge Road). Turn left, then right, SOUTH DEVON RAILWAY BUTTERFLY AND OTTER SANCTUARY.

Retrace your steps into Station Road. Turn right up the 196 steps to Holy Trinity. Leave the churchyard by the west gate and follow the lane ahead. When it divides, keep right and turn almost immediately right through a kissing gate. Keep the hedge on your left. Continue through the gate at the far end of the field and follow the enclosed path down to a road. Turn left for the Abbey.

Buckfast Abbey

Dissolved by Henry VIII, Buckfast Abbey was rebuilt in medieval style by French monks between 1882 and 1938. The abbey church (photograph above) is set amidst extensive gardens, including many medicinal plants. It is open to visitors.

From the abbey's car park, turn right and uphill, BUCKFASTLEIGH. The lane climbs steeply and then descends into Buckfastleigh. Turn right by Holne Court. Just beyond Silver Street is the launder that carried water to power the waterwheels of the old mills. Continue up Market Street. Turn left into Chapel Street and retrace your steps via the Globe Inn and Plymouth Road to the car park.

Holy Trinity Church

In the flower-filled churchyard is the 17th century Cabell tomb, distinguished by its iron bars and slated roof: it is the source of many legends concerning the wicked Squire Richard Cabell and his pack of hellish hounds who are said to haunt the moor. Certainly they inspired part of Arthur Conan Doyle's *The Hound of the Baskervilles*, Sherlock Holmes's most famous case.

Ashburton

Distance: 2km (1¹/₄ miles)

Well placed on the Exeter to Plymouth road, Ashburton's wealth was founded on trade, in wool, tin, corn and cattle, with a regular market and two annual fairs. It was made a borough in 1238 and in 1305 became one of Devon's four Stannary towns, where tin was assayed, weighed and coigned. Tin remained of major importance through to the 17th century and was traded in a smaller way into the 19th. Equally, the cloth industry developed from medieval times, with a series of mills along the banks of the river Ashburn. Prosperity has given Ashburton a great legacy of historic buildings. Many have 16th and 17th century cores behind handsome 18th and 19th century facades. Slate hung-houses, including the Card House in North Street (photograph above) and number 31 East Street with its fish scale slates, are a special feature.

Start from the car park behind the town hall. Face the Town Hall. On your right is a late 18th/early 19th century weaver's house, with a wool loft on the top floor similar to those of the weavers' cottages in Chapel Street, Buckfastleigh (page 33).

Divert right down Kingsbridge Lane, where the three storey early

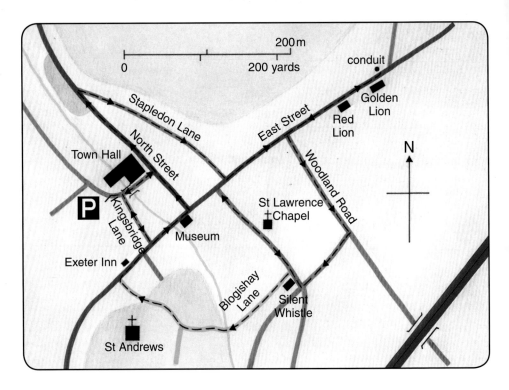

19th century houses are slate-hung. Retrace your steps. Turn right and cross the 18th century King's Bridge.

Turn left into North Street. The Town Hall was built as the market hall in 1850, of limestone with granite dressings, to replace the earlier wooden market hall. Lord Clinton's arms stand over the portico.

A building further along on the right was formerly the United Reform Church and before that the Congregational Church and adjacent schoolrooms. Turn right into Stapledon Lane, where the original cobbling is exposed in places. Local limestone and green volcanic ash predominate in the buildings.

Turn left into East Street. Among many historic buildings, number 31, dating from the early 18th century, is outstanding. Its ground floor has exposed stone rubble and its second storey is hung with ornamental hand-cut fishtail slates. These are probably original, but the plain slate-hanging and slated roof are thought to be later.

Further up the street and on the other side is the Red Lion (closed at the time of writing). It is 16th century in origin, but was remodelled in the 19th century. Next is the former Golden Lion, distinguished by its proud leonine motif and classic Georgian proportions. At one

Ashburton's Ale Tasting and Bread Weighing parade

time, Ashburton had thirty inns and public houses, but this number has been drastically reduced to single figures in a way all too familiar throughout Britain.

However, all Ashburton's surviving inns and its several bakeries are visited annually in the town's Ale Tasting and Bread Weighing ceremony, a colourful revival of a medieval custom designed to protect the public against unscrupulous traders.

Recross East Street to the stone conduit, part of the public water supply dating from 1797. The house behind was the Spread Eagle, one of many coaching inns that flourished in Ashburton.

Retrace your steps down East Street and turn left down Woodland Road with its attractive medley of building styles and materials.

Turn right past the former cattle market to The Silent Whistle. Since it opened in 1825, it has had four names, reflecting changes in Ashburton. Originally the Old Bottle, it changed to the Railway Inn when the South Devon Railway reached Ashburton in 1872. In 1962 the railway line closed and the pub adopted the apt name of The Silent Whistle, reverting to that name after a brief spell as the Fleece and Firkin. To the left is the old Station Yard and railway goods shed.

West Street

Divert right up St Lawrence Lane. St Lawrence Chapel is 13th century and served as Ashburton's Grammar School between 1593 and 1983. The tower was added early in the 16th century, the nave rebuilt in the 18th century and schoolrooms were added in the 19th and early 20th centuries. The Old Court House attached to the Chapel is late medieval, though altered in the 17th century. Now a private dwelling, it probably began as a priest's house.

Continue to the end of St Lawrence Lane. Opposite, on East Street, the Royal Oak is another late medieval building.

Now retrace your steps past St Lawrence Chapel and turn right along PUBLIC FOOTPATH BLOGISHAY LANE. This leads over the Ashburn and on past the churchyard to St Andrew's. Although the list of vicars stretches back to 1257, the church is mainly 15th century, with stately piers and a fine wagon roof.

Turn right into West Street, past a collection of historic buildings including the late medieval Exeter Inn (remodelled in the 18th century) to the Bull Ring where West, North and East Streets meet by the museum. The building is probably 17th century. The collections include items representative of Ashburton's ancient traditions, agriculture and industry.

Head up North Street. Number 1 is late medieval in origin. So too is Number 4, which was remodelled in the 16th/17th centuries. Its granite arch is similar to one in West Street.

Number 10 is late 17th/early 18th century and distinguished by its superb slate-hung, timber-framed front. It is known as the Card House because the slates are cut as hearts, clubs, diamonds and spades.

Turn left over King's Bridge to the start.